Usher

# Usher

## The Ultimate Entertainer

Marc S. Malkin

**Andrews McMeel
Publishing**

Kansas City

# To Mom . . . with all my love

www.andrewsmcmeel.com

98 99 01 02 RDC 10 9 8 7 6 5 4 3 2 1

Library of Congress Cataloging-in-Publication Data on file
ISBN: 0-8362-7840-2

## ATTENTION: SCHOOLS AND BUSINESSES

Andrews McMeel books are available at quantity discounts with bulk purchase for educational, business, or sales promotional use. For information, please write to: Special Sales Department, Andrews McMeel Publishing, 4520 Main Street, Kansas City, Missouri  64111.

## ACKNOWLEDGMENTS

The author would like to thank the following people: Dad, Grandma, Kevin, and the rest of my family; Steven LaGuardia and Andrew Colón for always listening; Clifford Hopkins; Caleb Crain; Peter Biskind; Howard Karren; Lauren Nussbaum; my photo editor, Jennifer Martin; my book editor, Nora Donaghy; and of course, my agent, Caroline Francis Carney.

## PHOTO CREDITS

**Pages 1, 6, 17, 19, 26, 27, 64, & 69:** Martha Gonzales/Outline; **pages 2, 16, & 43:** Michael Walls/Outline; **pages 44 & 46:** Thomas Lau/Outline; **page 7:** Mike Jones; **page 8:** Dark & Lovely; **pages 10, 13, & 20:** Ernie Paniccioli/Retna Ltd.; **pages 24, 31, 33, & 96:** Walter McBride/Retna; **page 49:** Steve Grantz/Retna; **pages 11, 14, 50, 87, & 94:** Kevin Mazur; **pages 38, 48, & 51:** Vincent Zuffante/Star File; **pages 40 & 41:** Todd Kaplan/Star File; **pages 5, 42, 65, & 75:** Jon Mead/Star File; **pages 22 & 47:** Dennis Van Tine/London Features; **pages 23, 73, 78, 84, & 90:** Anthony Cutajar/London Features; **pages 37 & 86:** George De Sota/London Features; **pages 45 & 68:** Ron Wolfson/London Features; **pages 5 & 56:** Nickelodeon/Craig Mathew; **pages 62 & 63:** Tommy Hilfiger Corp.; **page 60:** Ron Eisenberg; **pages 52, 53, 54, & 55:** Motown Café.

**Front cover photo:** Martha Gonzales/Outline
**Back cover photos:** Walter McBride/Retna; Tommy Hilfiger Corp., and Ron Wolfson/London Features

# Contents

# Welcome to the House of Usher

**S**hortly after his second CD, *My Way,* was released, Usher Raymond IV and a writer for *Vibe* magazine were driving through New York City in a limousine. Though Usher's one of the most down-to-earth celebrities around, he knew it would be easy to show the writer how successful he's become—how recognizable his face (as well as his sculpted physique) is. All

Usher had to do was stick his head out the limo's window. Within seconds, about two hundred fans surrounded the moving vehicle. The fans, mostly female, were ecstatic. "Usher's in there!" they screamed at the top of their lungs. "Usher's in there!"

So what exactly is the appeal of this young R&B singing sensation that makes fans so crazy that they're willing to step in front of a car just because he's in it? Why do girls want to be with him and why do guys want to emulate him or at least hang out with him—or become jealous of all his rabid female devotion? Why can't music fans get enough of this talented young star?

Discovered when he was barely a teen, Usher has become one of the biggest names in show business. He was just fourteen years old when LaFace Records discovered him on the TV talent show *Star Search*. LaFace's cofounder Antonio "L.A." Reid flew him to the record company's Atlanta headquarters from his home in Chattanooga, Tennessee, for a simple audition, and before he knew it, Usher was signed to the label that had already made international stars of artists like Toni Braxton, TLC, and LaFace's other cofounder, Kenneth "Babyface" Edmonds. Soon, he was working side-by-side with producer Sean "Puffy" Combs. Within two years, Usher was a sixteen-year-old with his first CD, *Usher*. And even though the first CD wasn't a

**Usher hangs with some of the models (left to right: Nikaya D. Brown, Kelly L. Robertson, and Talani N. Rabb) who appeared in his television commercial debut in Dark & Lovely's "Get Straight" advertising campaign.**

megahit, LaFace knew he had the potential of being the next Michael Jackson (a comparison that's been made plenty of times since Usher arrived on the scene). "Being a singer is what I've wanted since day one," he once declared. "Even when I was real young, people said that I sang all the time, so for me to give it up just because my first album didn't do everything I expected and wanted it to, ain't gonna happen."

Three years later, in September 1997, Usher's second album, *My Way*, was released. Within no time, Usher was a household name. By June 1998, *My Way* was certified triple platinum (meaning it had sold three million units). He's already toured with Puff Daddy, Janet Jackson, and Mary J. Blige. He made his acting debut opposite that other singing sensation, Brandy, on her hit TV show, *Moesha,* and fol-

This shot of Usher was snapped when he was filming a commercial for Dark & Lovely hair products. Advertising execs chose Usher to be in the campaign because he has such a huge following of young women.

lowed that up with appearances on *The Parent 'Hood* and *The Bold and the Beautiful*. Before he was even twenty years old, he had appeared on almost every talk show there is—and then some. And in December 1998, Usher

"I keep myself surrounded by p

makes his big-screen debut in the huge sci-fi flick *The Faculty*. And then there are those sexy Tommy Hilfiger and Dark & Lovely ads and commercials.

So, who is this guy born Usher Raymond IV? What makes him tick? What have been the most memorable moments in his life? And why have people from all over the world fallen in love with him?

Although it's easy to say Usher was born with his amazing talents and that it just comes naturally to him, there's more to it than that. His success is a combination of his hard work and determination, God-given talent, and the people who've recognized his gifts and nurtured him—including everyone from Puff Daddy and Jermaine Dupri to Babyface and, most important, his mom. These people want nothing more than to see Usher fly. "I keep myself surrounded by positive people," he told the *Indianapolis Star,* "and I realize that this can be a temporary or a lifelong experience. I'm definitely in it for longevity."

He's also "in it" in a big way. Usher once said that he dreams of becoming what he likes to call the "ultimate entertainer." He said, "I want to fill out all the different aspects from acting to dancing to producing to directing videos, directing movies. But definitely singing, dancing, and definitely writing."

It looks like nothing's going to stop this rising star from making his dreams come true. Here's your chance to share Usher's amazing journey from Chattanooga choirboy to international superstar.

sitive people".

"As a child, I **really** enjoyed getting up on that stage and basically showing off. I've always had a lot of **energy** to give, and I found something that was going to love me as much as I loved it, and that was **music**."

— Usher to the *Indianapolis Star*

# A Boy from Chattanooga

"As far as I can remember, I've **always** wanted to be a **singer**."

— Usher to *Sister 2 Sister* magazine

Usher was born Usher Raymond IV at four a.m. on October 14, 1978, in Dallas, Texas. From the time he was a baby until he was twelve years old, Usher, his mom, and younger brother, James, lived in Chattanooga, Tennessee, a city known for its breathtaking mountain views, Civil War monuments and memorabilia, the historic choo-choo train, and the world's largest freshwater aquarium. Although he has had no contact with his father since he was born,

## Usher's not the only celebrity to come from Chattanooga. Here are some others:

Actor Samuel L. Jackson

Women's professional
   basketball player Venus Lacey

Blues singer Bessie Smith

NBA superstar Gerald Wilkins

Opera diva Grace Moore

NFL greats Reggie White
   and Roy Oldham

Baseball pitcher Rick Honeycutt

Former U.S. ambassador to
   NATO David Abshire

Playwright Jim Wann

Actor Dennis Haskins (he plays
   Principal Richard Belding
   on *Saved by the Bell*)

Usher has always had a lot of family around him, including his grandmother (she's the one who first persuaded him to start baring more skin—and muscle—during his shows) and grandfather, and a lot of uncles. In one interview, Usher points out that he has one particular cousin who has really helped him out through the years—helping him navigate the sometimes-scary and overwhelming path from boyhood to manhood.

Usher attended the inner city Orchard Knob Elementary School and Dalewood Middle School. It was at Dalewood that Usher would really start showing signs that he was born to be a star. Teachers there still remember the times he wowed students and faculty with his amazing voice in the school's talent shows, how his music teacher encouraged Usher to sing (he even thought Usher should join the Chattanooga Boys

Choir—but Usher didn't), and how he was once a member of local singing group called New Beginnings. And Usher hasn't forgotten how much the school meant to him. Shortly after his first CD came out in 1994, he made a special trip to the school to visit his old friends and teach-

ers. Usher also visited Chattanooga in September 1995, when he coheadlined the "All-Star Homecoming Concert Classic," a benefit for the Mary Walker Foundation. Not surprisingly, today's students love to ask their teachers what they remember about Usher.

## Choirboy

While Usher was impressing his classmates during talent shows, he was also becoming a fixture at the St. Elmo Missionary Baptist Church in Chattanooga. His mom was the church youth choir's director, and when Usher was only nine years old she made him join the choir. And interestingly, she didn't even know her young son could sing. She put him in the choir because she wanted Usher to be active in the church and to stay out of trouble.

# "My mother's always been the pushing force behind the scene. She's always been the silent partner to keep me going."

— Usher to *Sister 2 Sister* magazine

At first, Usher wasn't really into spending his free time hanging around the church and singing. But it didn't take long for Usher to realize that he loved singing and was a born entertainer. "As a child," he told *Vibe* magazine, "you're not really worried about tomorrow because you got your mother to take care of you. When you get older, you start thinking, I got to do something with my life. I saw how my father was, and as an example of that I sort of said I'm not going to end up like that." (Usher's father isn't discussed by the family. "I don't care to talk about Usher's father," Usher's mom told *Vibe*. "He's never been a part of his life.")

**Usher and the main woman in his life, his mom and manager, Jonetta Patton.**

His church choir days have had an enormous impact on Usher that goes far beyond singing. Although he says he's not a very religious guy, he repeatedly credits God for giving him his talents. He feels God wants him to share his special gifts with the rest of the world. "I know that God has shined a light on me that is bright enough for the whole world to see," he told *MTV News.* "And I'm happy for that!" One time, he told a magazine that one of his all-time ideal dates is simply going to church with a girl.

But there's definitely no doubt which person has had the biggest influence on Usher—his manager, who happens to be none other than his mom, Jonetta Patton. Usher has absolutely no problem telling the world that his mom is his best friend, inspiration, and the driving force behind his amazing success. "We're very close," Usher bragged to *Sister 2*

*Sister* magazine. In an industry where even the biggest star is vulnerable—emotionally and monetarily—every celebrity wants to know there's at least one trustworthy person who's watching out for his or her own good. For Usher, that trusted confidante is his mother. "You know she's not going to let nothing happen to her baby," he says.

No one loves to make his mom proud more than Usher. He told *MTV News,* "I can give her anything I want now. I'm buying her cars, houses, jewelry, whatever." Even so, he emphasizes that the most important thing to him is the "love we share as a family, and the things she's taught me." When people comment on how nice and cool he is, Usher credits his mom for making sure that no matter how hard life could have gotten, he should remind himself that there were always positive things to be happy about. "It always helps to have someone behind you, and my mother was that person," Usher told the *Tacoma News Tribune,* a Washington state newspaper. "I encourage parents to stay with the kids."

Over time, his mom has encouraged Usher to take on more responsibility for his career choices. "Me and my mother have a very open relationship," he told *Interview.* "But these last few years, my mother has allowed me to make decisions for myself—to become a man." Guess you could say that Jonetta Patton is letting her superstar son do it his way!

# In the Beginning, There Was Music

Since the day he was born, Usher's been surrounded by music. His mom was always playing her records in the house

In September 1995, after making a **name** for himself with his first CD, Usher performed for the **first** time in his native Chattanooga. He told the *Chattanooga Times* that he **was already working** on his second album. At the time, it was called *The Book of Love.* And it was **supposed to be released in the spring of 1996.**

when he was growing up. "I grew up listening to soul singers like Marvin Gaye, Stevie Wonder, and Donny Hathaway—everybody my mother listened to," he says. Church was where he first performed, but he says, "Even before I started singing in church, I used to hum and sing with the radio."

Eventually that humming and singing would lead to bigger dreams of becoming what Usher

Usher **promises** to keep **lifting** up his **shirt** and taking **off** his shoes during his **shows**, but he told *MTV News* that he has stopped **dropping** his **pants**. Why? **"Too many** people are doing it. I think there's so **much** more.... There's a lot of people doing it, **so** I let that go."

likes to call "the ultimate entertainer." And for as long as he can remember he's been studying some of the greatest entertainment legends of all time. While Usher says he wants to be just like Michael Jackson, that doesn't mean he doesn't have other favorite artists. He credits the most famous artists of the past few decades as his biggest influences, including (in no particular order) Jackson, LL Cool J, Fred Astaire, Frank Sinatra, Donny Hathaway, Cab Calloway, Jackie "Mr. Excitement" Wilson, James Brown, Puff Daddy, Barry White, and Teddy Pendergrass. His favorite rapper of all time is the late Notorious B.I.G. And his all-time favorite song is Shirley Murdock's "As We Lay." "I study legends because I want to be a legend," Usher proclaims.

Growing up, Usher would do anything he could to learn about music. He told one writer that when he would attend sleepover parties he wouldn't play with the other kids. He'd be totally happy just sittin' by the radio and listening to music all night long. It was the only time, he says, that he had the chance to hear those sexy slow jams that radio stations didn't play during the day.

# Who's That Guy?
# The First CD

that forcing him to join St. Elmo's youth choir would get him started on his career path and change their lives forever.

As soon as Usher told his mom he wanted to be a performer, she did everything she could to help him fulfill his dreams. Whether he made it or not, she wasn't about to stop him from trying. "I have a passion for this," Usher told the *Indianapolis Star.* "As a child, I really enjoyed getting up on stage and basically showing off. I've always had a lot of energy to give, and I found something

Like most artists before him and all those to follow, Usher had to pay his dues to get a record deal. He did the talent shows, the church singing, and continually performed at school functions. But little did Usher's mom know

Usher was **discovered** by LaFace Records on the TV show *Star Search*. Other **celebrities** who were discovered on the **television** talent show include Rosie O'Donnell, Roseanne, Alanis Morissette and LeAnn Rimes.

Usher's first CD cover.

that was going to love me as much as I loved it, and that was music." His mom started entering Usher into all sorts of local talent competitions. He made his stage debut in a high school talent contest—even though he was only in *middle* school at the time—wowing everyone by singing Tevin Campbell's "Tomorrow."

Usher went on to win many talent contests, and in turn his mom became his manager. "When my mother started as my manager, she wasn't a full-time manager," Usher told *MTV News*. "It was something that she had taken up as a hobby or a study, working towards being a manager. But she put all her heart into this, as well as me as an artist, and it is great to see myself go through the next level and meet so many different people, but it means more to see my mother stop what she was doing in her life, and dedicate that time to getting me somewhere in my life."

At the time Usher was starting out, one of the biggest talent competitions was the TV show *Star Search,* where singers, comedians, dancers, and actors competed in front of a live studio audience. It was hosted by Ed McMahon, Johnny Carson's famed announcer and sidekick on *The Tonight Show.* Usher's mom entered him on the show in 1992. In no time, he became the show's reigning teen champion.

And it was *Star Search* that completely changed Usher's life. During one taping, there was a man in the audience named

Bryant Reid, an executive at LaFace Records, the huge record label that launched the careers of Toni Braxton, TLC, and Bobby Brown and was cofounded by his brother, Antonio "L.A." Reid, and Kenneth "Babyface" Edmonds. As soon as Bryant heard little fourteen-year-old Usher open his mouth and sing "End of the Road" by Boyz II Men (a LaFace group), he called L.A. The record mogul invited the young Usher to audition for him and some female staffers at LaFace's company headquarters in Atlanta. "I went to their office, sang the song again, and L.A. Reid asked me if I wanted a record deal," Usher told the *Los Angeles Times*. Obviously, L.A. knew right away that Usher had what it took to make it big—*really* big. L.A. told *Vibe* about the audition: "Usher picked out the young lady he thought was the prettiest, sang right to her, and won her heart."

What does Usher think L.A. saw? "They saw the marketability of this all-American kid, but they also liked my voice."

For her son to make it big, Usher's mom knew they'd have to leave Tennessee. She wanted Usher as close to LaFace as possible. As soon as the contracts were signed with LaFace, the family packed up and moved to Atlanta. She even canceled her son's next *Star Search* appearance because she wanted to get Usher to Atlanta pronto.

Immediately, Usher was meeting the biggest names in music. LaFace execs decided Usher would work best with Sean "Puffy" Combs, who was then known as a whiz kid producer responsible for helping to launch the careers of Mary J. Blige, Jodeci, and Heavy D. He's also the founder of Bad Boy Records, the label behind the late Notorious B.I.G., Faith Evans, Total, and 112. And many now know Puffy as a producer *and* a performer because of his multi-platinum debut album, *No Way Out,* and the subsequent Puff Daddy & the Family tour.

Usher and Puffy hit it off right away. In fact, Usher temporarily moved to New York City to live with Puffy so he could get as much guidance from his mentor as possible. During the eight months Usher lived with Puffy, the two got so tight that Puffy was known to refer to Usher as his little brother. Usher got to hang with hip-hop stars like Biggie Smalls (The Notorious B.I.G.) and Craig Mack. Even though Usher

could have lived a fast-track party life, he refused. It's not something he wanted or needed.

Puffy wanted only the best in the business to work on Usher's debut album. He enlisted the help of the industry's top producers and songwriters, including Jodeci's DeVane Swing, Al B. Sure!, and Dave "Jam" Hall.

LaFace was out to make Usher its next superstar. They got him on *The Oprah Winfrey Show* and a gig on the American Music Awards as part of the prestigious recording collective called Black Men United. His voice popped up on various sound tracks and compilation albums. In fact, his first single was not part of his debut album. It was the song "Call Me a Mack," which was on the sound track of the 1993 movie *Poetic Justice* (starring Janet Jackson and Tupac Shakur). It was released about a year before Usher's debut album.

Usher's self-titled debut album was released in 1994. LaFace was pushing Usher big-time. The marketing machine and promotion people were in full force. LaFace arranged a huge promotion with Teen Image deodorant and the Musicland record store chain. One hundred thousand coupons were packaged with the deodorant and could be used to get a LaFace sampler cassette featuring three Usher tunes along with four tracks from Toni Braxton's hugely successful self-titled CD. At the time, Usher told *Billboard* magazine that there were times during the making of the first CD when he didn't really understand what direction LaFace wanted his music to go in. "But I really understood it after the final mix," he said. "It all just came together." He was also confident that many different kinds of people would like his music. "I feel that my music will appeal to all sorts of crowds, despite my age," the then-sixteen-year-old said.

Unfortunately, it didn't. Despite one top-ten hit—"Think of You"—the CD was a commercial disappointment. Usher and most critics agree that the main reason the debut didn't sell well

was because he was singing "sexed-up" songs that dealt with ideas he couldn't relate to at such a young age. "Think of You" peaked at No. 8 on *Billboard*'s Hot R&B Singles Chart and the CD sold only about 35,000 units— definitely not enough to make him the household name that he is today.

"The first album I was young," Usher told *Vibe,* "maybe too young to be talking about making love to a girl, 'cause it wasn't really reality."

Although his sales weren't impressive, LaFace didn't give up on Usher. They knew he had what it took for stardom. With some more time and the right material, they said, there was nothing Usher couldn't do.

When Usher made his album debut, he was only sixteen years old. And like the typical sixteen-year-old, he was going through puberty. For him this reportedly meant a small battle with acne, and most troubling, a change in his voice. In fact, Usher has said, his voice actually began to change while he was still making his first CD. After the first CD failed and with his voice changed, there was a time that Usher thought he'd never sing again professionally.

Almost every male teen singing star experiences what Usher did in the beginning of his career. Every time a new teen has a hit, critics are quick to point out that no one knows what the future will bring because his voice is still developing. One recent example of this is Hanson. While the three brothers have enjoyed huge success with their debut album, *Middle of Nowhere,* the voices that the Hansons have now will soon change. But then there's Usher's idol, Michael Jackson. He went from child star to an adult singing sensation with

no problems whatsoever.

As always, Usher's mom was there to help him get through those tough times. She insisted that LaFace pick up the tab for the best voice lessons money could buy. "I kept telling the record company to hang in there with him," his mom has said. "I just wanted them to ride it out with us until his voice change was finished." Once Usher began to embrace his changing voice, nothing could stop him. "My voice

# *Usher* and *My Way* aren't the only places that you can hear Usher's smooth voice.

- In 1993--about a year before his debut album--Usher had a single called "Call Me a Mack" on the sound track of the 1993 movie *Poetic Justice.*

- In 1995, he recorded a holiday season jingle for Coca-Cola.

- He was one of several top musicians who was featured on the gold single "You Will Know," a song by the ensemble group Black Men United. The song was on the 1994 *Jason's Lyric* sound track.

- Usher's single "Dreamin'" was the first release from LaFace Records' 1996 Olympic album *Rhythm of the Games.*

- He appeared on Monica's debut 1995 platinum album, *Miss Thang,* in a duet remake of the hit single "Let's Straighten It Out." The song was also on the sound track for the 1995 movie *Panther.*

- Along with stars like Mariah Carey, Mase, Jay Z, Snoop Dogg, DMX, R.O.C., Too Short, Lil' Kim, Da Brat, Nas, Slick Rick, Keith Sweat, and Eight Ball, Usher lent his voice in 1998 to *My Way* producer Jermaine Dupri's debut album, *Life in 1472: The Original Soundtrack.*

- It's no surprise that you can also hear Usher on the sound track for *Soul Food*--Babyface and his wife, Tracey, produced the movie. It's the "Slow Jam" duet with Monica that's also on *My Way.*

- He also helps out his friend Shaquille O'Neal on the sound track for the basketball star's 1996 big-screen debut, *Kazaam,* with the song "I Swear I'm in Love."

- And if you want to feel like Usher's come home to you for the holidays, check out his 1993 tune "This Christmas" on the album *A LaFace Family Christmas.*

- Usher appears on the sound track for *Why Do Fools Fall in Love?,* a film about the late '50s doo-wop singer Frankie Lymon.

is a lot deeper now," Usher says today. "That's something that every man in the world goes through. Everybody has that vocal change. Whether you work with it or not is your decision." Usher decided to work with it.

Next up was finding the right team for his second CD. Usher knew it was more important than ever to find a producer who could help him break out with a major hit. Although the artist is the most important element of a CD, producers play a huge role. They are the behind-the-scenes people who are responsible for helping the artist find the right direction for a project and attracting the needed support from the record label.

Usher approached Puffy Combs about working together on his second CD, but Puffy was involved with other projects and couldn't give his full attention to another Usher project. (There were no hard feelings—after *My*

*Way* was released, Usher joined Puffy on his now-famous Puff Daddy & the Family tour.) So, Usher had to find another producer.

Even if Usher's second CD wasn't coming together as smoothly as he had hoped, he was still in demand after his first CD was released. While meeting with various producers and reportedly recording dozens of songs, Usher was tapped by Dallas Austin, another bigwig producer known for his work on hits for Madonna and TLC. Austin asked Usher to do a duet with R&B singer Monica on her debut album. The two young singers made an incredible remake of the hit song "Let's Straighten It Out." At the time, the *Los Angeles Times* compared Usher to a young Teddy Pendergrass. Usher explained that the soul he put into that song "came from listening to jazz and blues records."

Everyone got a kick out of watching Usher in the studio with Monica. "I had everybody in the studio laughing at me because I was singing with so much passion," he said. Usher was determined to make sure that the Usher they were hearing was not the same young man who had released a not-so-successful CD about a year before.

Usher's been the national spokesperson for the U.S. Department of Transportation's "Get Big on Safety" campaign. He's also participated in the NBA's "Stay in School" program. He's performed at several of the program's events to stress the importance of education.

Usher even approached Austin about working with him on his next CD, but like Puffy, Austin was already committed to other projects. Also, L.A. Reid reportedly wasn't overly enthusiastic about the supposed thirty-odd songs Usher had recorded during this period in preparation for the second CD. It was a tough time for Usher. But as always, his mom kept his spirits up, even when things looked like they were falling apart. "People were downing me and she said, 'Yo, you all can't do this to this kid,'" Usher told *Sister 2 Sister*. "'I'm not going to let you do this.'"

Usher kept pushing himself. "I still believed I had what it took," he remembers. "And LaFace kept the faith, too."

# Doing It His Way

Jackson, Toni Braxton, and TLC. Usher knew Jermaine already—Jermaine had done some, but not a lot, of work on Usher's debut album. "What happened was Jermaine Dupri hooked up a remix [of 'Think of You'] for me on my first album and I liked his vibe," Usher told *Tafrija* magazine. "So me and J. D. got together and I stayed with him for a couple of months to see what he was all about."

Usher did exactly what he had done with Puffy—he moved

next to meet with Usher was Jermaine Dupri, a producer known for working with the best in the business, including Michael *and* Janet

Usher named his *My Way* CD after his **favorite** Frank Sinatra song. He told *Entertainment Weekly* that he

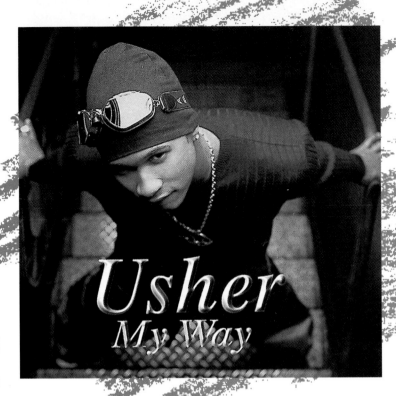

was **introduced** to Sinatra's **music** by his godfather, entertainer Ben Vereen. "It opened my mind up," Usher said. "I said, 'This **cat** is smooth. I want to be as **smooth.**' He was a **heartthrob**, he had a **million**-dollar smile, he was **charming**, and people just waited to hear his **every** word. And on top of that, his music was **great.**"

in with Dupri. They wanted to get to know each other and make sure they could work together. "We would go out a lot and just get a vibe for each other so that we could get a working relationship established," Usher says. "We have a great working relationship and I think Jermaine, by far, is the best person who has ever produced me."

Jermaine and Usher spent hours together every day, eating breakfast together and then just hanging out. Jermaine wanted to know everything about the young star-to-be so he could help him create an album that was totally real—that was completely about the *real* Usher. Jermaine would even tell Usher to call a girl on the phone so he could listen in and observe how Usher interacted with the ladies. Usher told *USA Today:* "It would have been easy for him to give me something that he felt would be a hit, but finding something that worked for me took time, and I thank him for taking it."

Usher and Jermaine's partnership was a perfect fit. "Jermaine's like my family," Usher says. And when the album was done, there could be only one name for it—*My Way.* Usher finally got to do things *his* way, and nothing could have summed the album up better than naming it after his favorite Frank Sinatra

**Usher perfomed at the gala opening of Disney's Animal Kingdom in Orlando, Florida.**

song. No one—especially Usher and Jermaine—wanted to see a repeat performance of the first CD. Usher took control this time, calling the shots and making sure everyone knew exactly what he wanted—even if people didn't agree with him. He was involved with every facet of *My Way*'s creation, especially making sure the lyrics were words he could relate to. He was a cowriter on five of the CD's tracks. "They were very open to what I suggested and at the same time brought me something new," he told *USA Today*. "You can hear the difference in my tone. It's just a little more grown-up. Usher is not a little kid anymore."

## "You Make Me Wanna . . ."

On July 14, 1997, "You Make Me Wanna . . ." was officially released as the first single off of *My Way*. Radio stations began playing it instantly and constantly. The song was a hit. Radio station switchboards lit up like crazy—listeners wanted more. (Interestingly, "You Make Me Wanna . . ." was the last song Usher recorded for the album.) Usher also became a familiar site on television. He did the talk-show circuit, and MTV and BET put the "You Make Me Wanna . . ." video in heavy rotation. The video was later nominated for an MTV Video Music Award for Best R&B Video. But the world would have to wait until September 16, 1997, to hear the rest of *My Way*. That was the day the album officially hit the stores in the United States. (The European release would come a few months later.) If there were any worries that *My Way* would have problems topping the charts, they were completely forgotten once the CD hit the stores.

*My Way* contains nine tracks (not including the extended version of "You Make Me Wanna . . ."). Jermaine Dupri produced six, Babyface two, and Sprague "Doogie" Williams one. It was executive produced by Dupri, Babyface, and L.A. Reid. It was definitely a team effort that made this CD so magical.

## Others involved included:

• Singer Shanice Wilson: She provides the backup vocals on "Bed Time."

• Monica: Usher's old friend didn't forget the "Let's Straighten It Out" duet he did with her on her debut platinum album in 1995. On *My Way,* she sang with Usher on the cover of Midnight Star's hit from 1983, "Slow Jam." This song also appears on the *Soul Food* sound track.

• The Isley Brothers: This oldies group's single "Footsteps in the Dark" is sampled on "One Day You'll Be Mine."

• And Lil' Kim lent him her rapping ways on "Just Like Me."

*My Way* wasn't the only thing on Usher's mind when he was in the studio. Not only did he help create one of the hottest albums of 1997, but with the help of a private tutor, he also earned his high school diploma at the same time!

# My Way

Usher was thrilled with the new CD. "It's not 100 percent R&B," Usher told *Sister 2 Sister*. "It's more like a new swing vibe, a combination of hip-hop and R&B." The world was getting to know Usher and his new sounds. Usher did exactly the right thing by releasing "You Make me Wanna . . ." as the album's first single. Not only does the song allow Usher to show off his smooth chords, but it's a brutally honest song about wanting to hook up with his girlfriend's friend. But despite the subject matter, Usher would never cheat on his girlfriend. "It was just a thought in my mind," Usher told *Interview* magazine. "I wanted to make her my girl, but I had a girl. Jermaine Dupri also had a similar experience, so we both wrote about it. We just exaggerated a bit to make the song more interesting." That's exactly what made Usher and Dupri work so well together—each took something from the other and combined it with his own experiences and made it the best possible tool to show off Usher's gifts.

Before *My Way* even hit the stores, fans and the media wanted to know more about the new

"*My Way* isn't vulgar or anything, but it does deal with real issues. It's about a young man entering manhood. It's my feelings."

—Usher to the *Orange County Register*

**Usher** had only **one** day to learn all those **dance** moves you see **him** do in the **video** for "You Make Me Wanna . . ."

grown-up Usher. LaFace made sure everyone had a chance to. He performed at "Back-to-School" showcases in high schools and at Boys and Girls Clubs across the country. (As a little kid, Usher would go to Boys and Girls Clubs when his mom was working.) He also appeared at Atlanta's Sisters Expo and health and beauty conventions. And he performed live at New York's Harlem Week celebration. Once everyone got a look at him performing, he became one of the most sought-after entertainers and sex symbols around. He was dubbed "The New King of the Stage." The media

In less than three months, 500,000 copies of *My Way* were sold. "You Make Me Wanna . . ." spent eleven weeks on top of *Billboard*'s Hot R&B Singles chart, tying the 1992–1993 record set by none other than the Whitney Houston classic "I Will Always Love You." LaFace was so happy with Usher's success that they threw a huge surprise party for Usher and Jermaine Dupri—complete with Cristal champagne, catered food, and red balloons—at their Atlanta offices. Usher was left speechless. "I . . . I, man, they got me," was the only thing a shocked Usher was able to tell a reporter from the *Atlanta Journal Constitution*. And in England, Arista—LaFace's parent company—arranged for Usher to perform at London's Fashion Café on February 4, 1998, to celebrate an amazing 200,000 British sales of

couldn't get enough of him. Usher and his chiseled physique were all over magazines and newspapers. Web sites sprung up faster than some of Usher's fancy foot work. Usher had truly arrived.

After Puff Daddy caught Usher performing in September 1997 on *Showtime at the Apollo,* he insisted Usher join him on his now-famous Puff Daddy & the Family tour. Usher began his six-week, thirty-one-city, thirty-six-show stint with Puffy on November 7, 1997. He got to share the stage with a load of stars, including Puffy, Busta Rhymes, Lil' Kim, Jay-Z, Foxy Brown, the Lox, and Kid Capri. Usher says touring with Puffy has been one of the high points of his career. "We are a family, the Puff Daddy family, hip-hop history to the fullest, from rap to hip-hop to soul," Usher told the *Courier-Journal,* a Louisville, Kentucky, newspaper, during one of the tour's many stops. "If you want a history lesson in hip-hop music, you'd better come." And, Usher insisted, "Be there early because I come on first." He thinks Puffy gave Usher the first twenty minutes of the concert because his performances are so squeaky clean. "I don't have a lot of profanity in my show," Usher said, adding that if he were a parent, he wouldn't let his kids stay after his performance "because it can get kind of crazy."

But it would be a Brit who prevented "You Make Me Wanna . . ." from reaching No. 1 on the charts.

Something happened not long after the release of the single that nobody ever could have predicted. Princess Diana was tragically killed in a car accident. Her close friend, Sir Elton John sang "Candle in the Wind" at the princess's funeral. John immediately released the tribute as a charity benefit single. Despite its huge success, "You Make Me Wanna . . ." never made it to No. 1 on *Billboard*'s Hot 100 chart because it was released at about the same time as "Candle in the Wind," a song that would go on to to be the biggest-selling single of

"You Make Me Wanna . . ." in just three days. He was also given a silver compact disc to mark the occasion. The actual *My Way* CD was released on February 9, 1998, in England.

all timo. Although Usher would have loved hitting No. 1, he was all right with Elton John dominating the charts. "Hey, I pay my respects to Princess Diana," he said at the time to the *Arizona Republic*. "And that's a great place to be, number two. To stand next to someone so great as Elton John—it's a thrill."

On February 6, 1998, LaFace proudly announced that *My Way*'s second single, "Nice & Slow," had hit No. 1 on *Billboard*'s Hot 100 and R&B Singles charts. At the time, *My Way* was still No. 4 on the *Billboard* 200 and R&B Album charts. The video for "Nice & Slow" was directed by top director Hype Williams. And the word is that Usher took French lessons because the video was shot in the city of love—Paris.

Usher had been a bit worried when *My Way* was about to be released. He was nervous about holding his own. But in the end, his

**Usher and his back-up dancers during a Puff Daddy & the Family tour stop in Worcester, Massachusetts.**

the highest-ever number of listeners for any R&B single. The previous record holder was Joe's "All the Things (Your Man Won't Do)," which hit fifty million in April 1996.

*My Way's* second single, "Nice & Slow," was No. 1 on the R&B chart for eight weeks. Less than eight months after its release,

confidence won out. "There was a little pressure," he says, "but I believed in it all the way."

*My Way* reached No. 1 on the R&B chart and No. 4 on the pop chart. "You Make Me Wanna . . ." reached more than 50.7 million R&B radio listeners within three months of its release, giving it

*My Way* had been certified triple platinum (meaning it had sold three million copies), and it shows no signs of slowing down.

By July 1, 1998, the third single, "My Way," was certified gold by selling 500,000 units.

**Guess** who was one of the **first people** to tell Usher how **sexy** he was and urged him to hit the gym? His grandmother. "She told me, 'You *sex-y*--why don't you go ahead and **work** out?" Usher remembered in *Rolling Stone*. "She didn't have a problem with it and my grandmother's old."

# Grammy Nominee

Soon, Usher would be receiving some of the music industry's biggest awards and nominations. First, he was asked to help announce the fortieth annual Grammy Award nominations at New York City's Radio City Music Hall along with other performers such as Paula Cole, Shawn Colvin, Fiona Apple, Wyclef Jean, and Diane Krall. Little did he know that he would be one of the nominees announced that day. "You Make Me Wanna . . ." earned him a nomination for Best Male R&B Vocal Performance. "I'm ecstatic and surprised by this nomination," Usher said at the time. "I attribute this honor to all the hard work my record company, my manager, and all of the people who work with me have given to this project." The competition was fierce: R. Kelly for "I

Believe I Can Fly," Kenny Lattimore for "For You," Luther Vandross for "When You Call on Me/Baby That's When I Come Runnin'," and Curtis Mayfield for "Back to Living Again." J. Freedom du Lac, the pop music critic for the *Sacramento Bee*, predicted that the award was a

When Usher **appeared** as a presenter for the fortieth annual Grammy Awards at Radio City Music Hall in New York City, he was seen by an estimated 1.5 billion viewers in 195 countries.

"two-man race between teen sensation Usher and the enigmatic Kelly." R. Kelly nabbed the award. But just like the time he was outdone by Elton John's "Candle in the Wind," Usher was no sore loser. In fact, he says he wants R. Kelly to collaborate with him on his next album.

Usher didn't win, but the nineteen-year-old was in amazing company on Grammy night. The list of nominees included Usher's first producer, Puffy (in seven categories, including one for producer of the year), Mary J. Blige, Wu-Tang Clan, Busta

**Even though Usher rehearsed as a presenter for the fortieth annual Grammy Awards, he was a little embarrassed when he called music legend Bob Dylan "Bill" during the show.**

**Usher hung out with Wyclef Jean when the two artists helped announce nominations for the fortieth annual Grammy Awards.**

Rhymes, LL Cool J, Will Smith, Tina Turner, and, for spoken albums, author Maya Angelou and comedian Chris Rock.

The night was much more than just an awards show for Usher. He had helped announce the nominees; he was greeted by screaming fans and paparazzi as he made his way across the red carpet into Radio City Music Hall;

he was a nominee himself; and he was a presenter that night, too. Although Usher was a bit embarrassed when he accidentally called music legend Bob Dylan "Bill" when he was announcing nominations for Album of the Year ("Everybody has a bad day," he said), the show would only help spread Usher fever around the world. As a presenter, he had an estimated 1.5 billion viewers in 195 countries with their eyes glued on him.

Before he was even twenty years old Usher was presenting at the Grammys alongside such famous musicians as Vanessa Williams, Gloria Estefan, Jewel, Erykah Badu, Wyclef Jean, LL Cool J, Maxwell, Puffy, Aretha Franklin, Patti LaBelle, and the group that gave Usher his life-changing LaFace audition song,

Boyz II Men. And Calvin Klein, who dressed Puffy, Babyface, and Meredith Brooks that night, insisted on dressing Usher, too.

The week leading up to the Grammy Awards was a busy time for Usher. Being one of the hottest superstars around meant practically everyone in the industry wanted to meet him. And if they couldn't meet him, they wanted to at least see him. Usher went to dozens of parties that were given throughout the Big Apple for the Grammys. Usher's old friend and producer, Puffy Combs, threw a party just for him at his famous downtown restaurant, Justin's.

And the president of Arista (LaFace's parent company), Clive Davis, personally invited Usher to perform at Arista's gala party at the chic five-star Plaza Hotel.

Who else performed? Whitney Houston, Aretha Franklin, Mary J. Blige, Sarah McLachlan, The Fugees' Lauryn Hill, Puffy, Boyz II Men, and Wyclef Jean.

**Usher helped announce the nominees for the fortieth annual Grammy Awards at Radio City Music Hall in New York City with other artists such as Shawn Colvin, Fiona Apple, Wyclef Jean, and Paula Cole. Little did he know that he was one of the nominees.**

**Usher shows off his Soul Train Award for Best R&B/Soul Single for a Male in February 1998.**

Not long after the Grammys, Usher began touring with Mary J. Blige, one of his all-time favorite singers. (This wasn't the first meeting for Usher and Blige. The two had met years before when Usher was working with Puffy on his first album.) The up-and-coming group Next also toured with them. The tour started March 25 at Detroit's Fox Theater and included nineteen concerts. Usher got a lot of attention for the tour. The rave reviews rolled in. MTV did a special on the tour.

And on July 9th he began his gig as Janet Jackson's opening act on the North American leg of her *Velvet Rope* world tour. They hit forty-six cities with fifty-one concerts. The tour ended in October with a live concert broadcast on HBO from Madison Square Garden. "I love the stage, to dance and perform," Usher told one reporter. "The stage is my first love." And he's certainly proved it.

Just a few days before the Grammys, Usher had to be at another awards show—this time it was in Los Angeles on February 27 for the twelfth annual Soul Train Music Awards. Usher won in the R&B/Soul Single, Male category for "You Make Me Wanna . . ." and also performed during the show. Even though Usher had some problems during his performance—he had trouble tearing off his shirt because the sleeves were still buttoned at the cuffs, and someone had to come on stage to give him his mike—he remained the consummate performer, smiling through the whole performance.

Other big winners of Soul Train Awards were Erykah Badu, The Notorious B.I.G., Puffy, and Dru Hill.

It was also in February that *Ebony* featured Usher as one of ten "Ebony Men on the Move." The piece featured men whom the magazine's editors thought were at the tops of their fields. And this was no minor list—others named were activist minister Dr. Robert M. Franklin Jr., Federal Communications Commission Chairman William E. Kennard, musician/composer Anthony Davis, actor Djimon Hounsou (the star of Steven Spielberg's *Amistad*), attorney and presidential appointee to the Federal Reserve Board of Governors Roger W. Ferguson Jr., Major

**Usher arrives with his backup at the Soul Train Awards at the Shrine Auditorium in Los Angeles on February 27, 1998.**

League Baseball executive Ricky Clemons, visual artist Andre White, farming activist John W. Boyd Jr., and Miami Heat superstar point guard Tim Hardaway. Usher may have been the youngest on the list, but he definitely was one of the bigger household names.

**Usher met one of his idols, Bobby Brown, at the Soul Train Awards.**

With all this success at such a young age, Usher could have turned into a spoiled star with an out-of-control ego and attitude. But he has remained completely grounded. It probably has a lot to do with the people he's surrounded himself with. He's made sure they're truly out there looking after him. Usher also makes sure to remind himself again and again how lucky he's been—how not everyone with big dreams gets to experience them. "Nobody's going to be on top forever," he told *Rolling Stone* rather modestly. "But when you're there, I say just love it. And I love it."

He's so down to earth that he even once called a reporter who'd had to postpone an interview because of her dental surgery. "Unlike several other so-called celebrities who were inconvenienced because I had to be in the

dentist chair and couldn't interview them, Usher called to find out how I was doing," writer Debi Fee wrote in *Fresh!* magazine. "We need more people like Usher in the business."

He also makes sure to give back to the community. He's involved with a bunch of chari ties, especially children's organizations like Boys and Girls Clubs. Usher himself would go to Boys and Girls Clubs after school when his mom was working. He's also served as a national spokesperson for the U.S. Department of Transportation's "Get Big on Safety" campaign. And being the huge basketball fan that he is, he helped out the NBA with its "Stay in School" program by performing for thousands of students nationwide to emphasize the importance of education. A one-shot appearance at New York City's Motown Café also turned into a benefit for children. Fans were asked to donate to a toy drive for underprivileged kids.

# A Day in the Life of Usher

**S**hortly after *My Way* was released, the Motown Café in New York City invited Usher to come to the restaurant to meet with his fans, sign some autographs, and donate a pair of his sneakers to its musical memorabilia collection. Here are some exclusive behind-the-scenes shots.

**Usher arrives at the Motown Café in New York City (top).**

**Dozens of fans came out to see Usher. Here, he's hustled upstairs to give a pair of sneakers to the Café (left).**

**Usher takes center stage (above).**

**Usher teases the crowd by showing them his six-pack (right).**

He gets ready to show off his physique (left).

Usher's no shy guy (below).

He makes sure to autograph his poster before he leaves (right).

Before he catches a chill, Usher puts on a Motown jacket to sign autographs and meet his fans (below).

# Must-See Usher TV

**In one of his many television appearances, Usher performed on Nickelodeon's *All That!***

*The Twelfth Annual Soul Train Music Awards*
*The Billboard Music Awards*
*Dick Clark's New Year's Rockin' Eve*
*The Oprah Winfrey Show*
*The Keenan Ivory Wayans Show*
*Vibe TV*
*The Chris Rock Show*
Nickelodeon's *Big Help-A-Thon*
Nickelodeon's *All That!*
*The Tonight Show with Jay Leno*
*Live with Regis and Kathie Lee*
MTV's *Fashionably Loud*
MTV's *House of Style*
*Showtime at the Apollo*
*The American Music Awards*
*Breaking Out—The Concert*
(a pay-per-view special)

this is one star the camera loves and can't get enough of. Usher has appeared on TV countless times. Highlights include:
*The Fortieth Annual Grammy Awards*

VH-1's *Before They Were Rock
    Stars II*
*The Magic Hour*
*The Howie Mandell Show*
MTV's *FANatic*
*Later*

"I've accomplished a lot of things already. But I still have my whole life ahead of me, and more to do. I want to keep making records, performing live, and writing songs. I also plan to produce myself and other artists, and someday become a really good and successful actor."

— Usher, when he was only eighteen

His acting and commercial appearances include:
    *Moesha*
    *The Parent 'Hood*
    *The Bold and the Beautiful*
    Dark & Lovely and
    Tommy Hilfiger commercials

# The Acting Usher

Just like some of his idols—especially Michael Jackson and Frank Sinatra—Usher wants to be known not only as a singer, but also as an actor. Usher's never taken an acting class in his life, but that certainly hasn't stopped him from getting some terrific roles.

## Moesha

It wasn't too long after *My Way* was released that Usher found himself hanging out with Brandy on the set of her hit UPN show, *Moesha*. But he wasn't merely checking out the cute singer-actress. Usher got something more—he snagged a recurring role on the show.

On October 14, 1997, Usher made his highly anticipated acting debut on *Moesha*. He played Jeremy, the high school football team captain who has big dreams of going into politics. He and Moesha meet after Moesha and her longtime steady, Q (played by Fredro Starr), break up. Even if there's a romantic chemistry between Moesha and Jeremy, the two of them don't really get serious because she's wary of getting into another relationship.

Usher says the people responsible for *Moesha* sent him a script as soon as they learned he wanted to act. *"Moesha* had been requesting me for a while," he remembers. "They sent me a script. They flew me out and I read for the part. They said I passed with flying colors."

And once he was on the set, the writers had a great time creating Jeremy. In fact, the characters on the show loved to talk about how much Jeremy looks like—you guessed it—Usher. In fact, at the end of his and Moesha's first date, Jeremy sings "You Make Me Wanna . . ." to her.

"He was mimicking Usher," Usher told *Jet*. "People [on the show] always tell Jeremy that he looks like Usher. Jeremy says, 'He's all right.' He's sort of jealous because Moesha likes Usher a lot."

And as it so often happens with other celebrities who have worked together, there were rumors that Usher and Brandy had more going on than just a working relationship. But both artists insist that they're just good friends. "Brandy and I kicked it and stuff," he told the teen newspaper *Harlem Overheard*. "We were just friends, though. I keep all business away from pleasure." But Usher helped fuel rumors by telling *Seventeen* magazine how he once took Brandy to the Waffle House in Atlanta. For the record, Brandy says her only serious boyfriend has been Wanya Morris of Boyz II Men. They were together for about a year and a half.

Although there are no plans right now for Usher to return to *Moesha,* no one has ruled out future Jeremy appearances. If nothing else, viewers can still catch Usher on *Moesha* reruns.

## The Bold and the Beautiful

*The Bold and the Beautiful* is Usher's mom's favorite soap opera. So it should come as no surprise that Usher was able to land a choice role on the soap in June 1998 for eight episodes. He played Raymond, a singer who was friends with Amber Moore (played by Adrienne Frantz) when she lived in Atlanta before she and her family moved to Los Angeles (where *The Bold and the Beautiful* takes place). Amber's boyfriend, Rick Forrester (played by Jacob Young), is not thrilled when Raymond comes to town—especially when Amber helps Raymond get a gig performing at a local club. As usual in soap land, things don't go as smoothly as everyone intends. Amber is crushed when Raymond unexpectedly leaves town because he gets an opportunity to tour with a major music star. Amber also discovers she is pregnant.

Usher sang "My Way" and the "Slow Jam" duet with Amber on the soap. Those appearances helped to solidify his popularity around the world. CBS's *The Bold and the Beautiful* airs every day in more than ninety-eight countries, reaching at least 450 million viewers worldwide.

**Usher played himself on *The Parent 'Hood.***

# The Parent 'Hood

Being on the WB's *The Parent 'Hood* on February 6, 1998, was no stretch for Usher. He got to play himself. The plot went like this: Zaria (played by Reagan Gomez-Preston) was having a huge sleepover party for her seventeenth birthday. The night's highlight was going to the Winter Jam, an all-star show starring Puff Daddy, Busta Rhymes, Mase, and, yes, Usher. (Earlier that day, Zaria had won tickets to the concert and backstage passes in a radio contest.) Zaria's parents were footing the bill for a limo and dinner at Planet Hollywood, too. But as luck would have it, the Big Apple gets hit with one of its biggest snowstorms ever and everyone—Zaria, her friends, and her family—is trapped in the house. And to make matters even worse, the power goes out and there's no food in the fridge. But in the end Usher comes through. He shows up at Zaria's house (the radio station had given him her

Usher played himself on one episode of *The Parent 'Hood,* the WB show starring comedian Robert Townsend.
Usher's favorite movie is *The Five Heartbeats,* which starred--Robert Townsend!

address) because he didn't want her to have a bad birthday. Zaria's birthday ends on the best note of all—Usher singing "You Make Me Wanna . . ." in her living room.

Like the Brandy rumors that started after his work on *Moesha,* some folks speculated that Usher and Reagan Gomez-Preston had hooked up. Again, camps for both stars deny this and insist they're just friends.

## The Faculty

In late 1998, Miramax—the huge film company known for launching the career of Quentin Tarantino and revitalizing the popularity of teen horror flicks with hits like *Scream* and *Scream II*—was preparing to release a movie called *The Faculty.* The release date was set for December 25, 1998, under Miramax's Dimension Films division on 2,500 screens nationwide.

**Usher was upset one day when he returned to the Austin, Texas, set of *The Faculty* to find that a director's chair with his name on it had been stolen by a fan.**

The film was shrouded in secrecy. Not much was known about it except that it was written by Kevin Williamson, the creator of the *Scream* movies and *Dawson's Creek*, and directed by Robert Rodriguez, who previously directed *From Dusk Till Dawn*. It has a huge cast of today's young stars—including Usher (who plays a not-so-friendly football player named Gabe), along with Jordana Brewster, Clea DuVall, Laura Harris, Josh Hartnett, Shawn Hatosy, Elijah Wood, and some established actors like Salma

Hayek, Famke Janssen, Piper Laurie, Christopher McDonald, Bebe Neuwirth, Robert Patrick, and Jon Stewart.

Dimension describes the film as a sci-fi flick that follows a group of students at Herrington High who discover something that, by comparison, makes the school lunch special seem normal. "The thriller," the film company announced, "proves that you were right to suspect your teachers might be from another planet."

Even with such a famous cast, all eyes seemed to be on Usher. During the shoot in Austin, Texas, in late spring 1998, Dimension had to keep Usher's role secret because they were nervous that fans would invade the sets and interrupt filming. But fans nevertheless found out Usher was in town shortly after he arrived,

because the singer was seen at a local record store with designer Tommy Hilfiger. The *Austin American-Statesman* reported that Usher bought all six of the store's copies of *My Way* to give his costars as presents.

**Usher takes a break while shooting Tommy Hilfiger's back-to-school ad campaign on the Austin film set of *The Faculty*.**

So, why was Usher with Tommy Hilfiger? As one of *The Faculty's* cast members, Usher was in a Hilfiger ad campaign for his Tommy Jeans line. After it was decided that Hilfiger would dress the entire cast for the movie, Dimension and Tommy Hilfiger Corp. embarked on a $30 million joint marketing and promotional effort. Previously, the most aggressive marketing effort by Miramax for a film opening was $15 million for Dimension's *Scream II*. Usher, along with Brewster, DuVall, Harris, Hartnett, Holstoy, Wood, and Kidada Jones (Quincy Jones's daughter and an extra in the film), all modeled Tommy Jeans apparel in a back-to-school campaign. "This is not about using models," Hilfiger told the *Hollywood Reporter,* a show-business trade magazine. "It's

**Usher struck up a friendship with Tommy Hilfiger when they shot the designer's back-to-school ad campaign.**

about using real personalities." The campaign was shot on the movie's Austin set. Usher can be seen in magazine ads as well as in commercials on MTV, VH-1, BET, and Comedy Central.

## Coming Attractions

Usher wants to have his own TV sitcom one day. That may happen sooner rather than later. According to some magazines, Usher has already started work on his own sitcom costarring gospel artist Kirk Franklin. In one

# One of Usher's favorite things to do is to watch *Pink Panther* cartoons.

report, Usher apparently has said that he hopes the show will be on the air in the spring of 1999. Reportedly, Franklin plays a washed-up pop star who's trying to rebuild his life in his hometown neighborhood. Usher costars as a character who dreams of being a huge star just like Kirk's character had been at one time.

Movie scripts keep coming his way, too. According to news reports, Usher is considering a part in an upcoming Eddie Murphy movie. And according to a report in *Billboard,* Usher also plans to write movies and produce them as well. A spokesperson for Usher told the magazine, "He's a true artist and not closed to any level of the entertainment industry."

# Kiss and Tell

relationships, dating, and what he looks for in a girlfriend—even though he's too busy to have one at the moment.

## Usher on Relationships

I s it the sight of his sculpted body? Could it be that adorable smile and those puppy-dog eyes? Maybe it's those smooth dance moves. And, of course, there's that voice. It's probably the complete package: the six-pack, smile, eyes, personality, dance steps, and vocals. But what does it take to make Usher go crazy for a woman? Here's Usher on love,

Having a girlfriend is difficult for Usher right now. In one interview he talked about a girlfriend whom he broke up with when he was seventeen. He cared about her, but he couldn't give the relationship the time and attention it deserved. "For me to have a steady girlfriend is impossible,"

> "I'm **prepared** to search **all around** the world for a potential **girlfriend**-- absolutely anywhere!"

—Usher to *Bliss* magazine

he told *react*. "Having a girlfriend comes with responsibilities. You have to spend lots of quality time together. I'm just trying to live my life and find out what I want to do. I'd like to get married one day, but I've got so much ahead of me."

Sex is definitely not Usher's main objective when it comes to dating. He says he's happy having some good conversation. "All guys are not motivated by sex," he promises.

# Usher on the Rules of Attraction

Although he doesn't have a girlfriend now, Usher still loves all the attention he gets from his female fans. He really thrives on seeing thousands of young women screaming and dancing at his shows. "They all put their hands up and I reach to touch as many as I can and they start screaming," he says. And even if he seems to pick out a special fan or two in the audience with a smile or a wink, he says he can't really concentrate on one particular person in the audience because he has to stay completely focused on his singing and dancing.

Usher has dated all types of young women of all different races. Although he has said looks aren't that important to him, he has also been known to rattle off some physical characteristics that really get him going, especially full lips. He likes a woman who takes care of herself. "I think she should have her nails manicured and keep herself clean, whether that means bathing regularly or just making sure she gets rid of the boogies from her nose," he told *TV Hits*, a British magazine. The magazine also quoted him as saying that he likes seeing a young woman get all dressed up—especially if she's in a skirt with a slit up its side. And he thinks actress Halle Berry and singer Scary Spice (Melanie Brown of the Spice Girls) are very sexy. "There are others," he says, "but those two are at the top of my list."

But Usher doesn't appreciate someone wanting to date him just because he's a star. "They have to like me for me, not just because I'm an artist," he says. "See, I'm always trying to keep it real."

Many people might assume Usher could date anyone he wanted, but that hasn't always been his experience. His inspiration for the song "One Day You'll Be Mine" came from a time when he wanted to date a girl who already had a boyfriend. "I didn't have a girlfriend, but she had a man," he says. "I understood because I'm not a cheating man. . . . If I had a girlfriend I would never cheat on her."

## The Dating Game

Drive-in movie theaters, being such a rarity today, are a special treat and Usher will make sure to find one when he's in the mood. He says he loves the idea

Usher loves butterscotch candies. He joked with supermodel Rebecca Romijn on MTV's *House of Style* that he likes sucking on the candy while talking with a girl. "That's a definite turn-on," he laughed.

> "I don't do drugs, and I don't have people around me who do drugs. I learned that you really got to watch the people you keep around you."

— Usher to *Vibe*

of sitting with his date in his shiny black Porsche, with the top down, watching a flick—and the stars—at an old-fashioned drive-in.

And Usher's definitely no cheap date. He once took a young woman on a one-day, three-city date. They had breakfast in Atlanta, lunch in Las Vegas, and dinner in Los Angeles.

As for those rumors that Usher has dated Brandy, Monica, and *The Parent 'Hood*'s Reagan Gomez-Preston, everyone close to them says they're just friends.

# Usher's Idols

**U**sher once said, "I've done a lot of studying, everything from rap, reggae, soul, rhythm, and blues—even country and classical. I can flip on any of those. Mostly, I just want to show my diversity, that I can rap, I can sing, I can dance." So, who's helping him achieve these dreams? Here's the lowdown on some of the artists he often names as his idols, mentors, and inspirations:

## The Jackson 5

These five brothers—Jackie, Tito, Jermaine, Marlon, and Michael—from Gary, Indiana, were one of the biggest pop groups of the 1970s. Some of their early hits include "I Want You Back," "ABC," "The Love You Save," and "I'll Be There." From day one, critics and fans agreed—Michael, the youngest (he was only eleven when the group was started by their dad, Joe), was the most talented and would probably be a *huge* star. Just like Usher, Michael wowed audiences not only with his voice, but with his incredible dance moves as well. Usher first heard "I Want You

Back" (the song was a hit in 1970—eight years before Usher was born) when he was watching a rerun of the Jackson 5 cartoon series on TV. "When I heard that song I was inspired; I wanted to sing just like Michael, to be like Mike," he says.

## Michael Jackson

After the Jackson 5 broke up, Michael went on to become "The King of Pop." His *Thriller* from 1982 became the best-selling album of all time. It sold twenty million copies in the United States alone. And it was Michael (whose signature style included one gloved hand) who got the whole country moonwalking. "My real ultimate is Michael," Usher says. "I really would like to be compared to him some day because he's the greatest." Not surprisingly, Usher loves to perform a medley of Jackson 5 and Michael Jackson hits during his shows.

## Frank Sinatra

You probably heard a lot about Frank Sinatra after his death in May of 1998. For decades, Sinatra was one of show business's most respected and loved entertainers. Like Usher, he began as a young singer, but later had a huge career as an actor as well. He even won an Oscar for Best Supporting Actor in 1953's *From Here to Eternity*. "I discovered him through [godfather] Ben Vereen," Usher told *Entertainment Weekly*. "It opened my mind up. I said, 'This cat is smooth. I want to be as smooth.' He was a heartthrob, he had a million-dollar smile, he was charming, and people just waited to hear his every word. And on top of that, his music was great."

# Donny Hathaway

Usher often cites Hathaway, a composer and vocalist from the '70s, as one of his favorite artists. A St. Louis native born in 1945, Hathaway is credited with influencing almost every African-American singer in recent decades. His first Top Ten R&B hit was "You've Got a Friend," a duet with Roberta Flack. Sadly, Hathaway committed suicide when he was thirty-three. "Donny Hathaway is the greatest singer in the world," Usher has said, adding, "I like those deeper, darker tones."

# Marvin Gaye

This singer and composer emerged in the '60s and '70s as one of the most popular R&B and soul artists ever. He had dozens of Top Ten hits and is known not only for his smooth romantic ballads, but for some more sexually charged hits. One of his most famous tunes was his last, "Sexual Healing." Tragically, Gaye was fatally shot by his father in an argument in 1984.

# Stevie Wonder

Like Usher, Stevie Wonder began his career at an early age—thirteen to be exact. And his career hasn't stopped since. Since he started recording in 1963, he's had dozens of hits, including "Superstition," "My Cherie Amour," and "You Are the Sunshine of My Life." He is one of the most respected soul singers ever, although he's had some more commercial success with his pop and rock songs. You most recently heard him singing "True To Your Heart" with 98° on the *Mulan* sound track.

## Jermaine Dupri

Like Puff Daddy, Jermaine Dupri is one of the most sought-after producers in the music business. He's worked with many top artists, including Aretha Franklin, Mariah Carey, Mase, Kris Kross, Da Brat, MC Lyte, TLC, Whodini, Lil' Kim, Dru Hill, and Aaliyah, and on the sound tracks for *Men in Black* and *Love Jones,* among many others. Dupri is credited with helping *My Way* become the hit it is today. (He's one of three executive producers.) In July 1998 Dupri released his debut album, *Life in 1472.* Usher appears on *1472.*

## Puff Daddy

Sean "Puffy" Combs began his career in 1990 as an intern at Uptown Records in New York City. He was then still attending Howard University, but eventually he dropped out to work full-time. Before long he was helping direct the careers of Mary J. Blige, Jodeci, and Heavy D. He started his own label, Bad Boy, in 1993. In 1997, his company reportedly made about $150 million. Usher first met him when he was just starting out—Puffy produced Usher's self-titled debut album in 1994. Usher praises Puffy for all that he taught him about the business and creative sides of the music world. "He's a genius," Usher says, adding, "I think he has a lot to offer everyone coming up in the music industry." Puffy personally invited Usher to join him on the now-famous Puff Daddy & the Family tour in 1997.

## Babyface

Kenneth "Babyface" Edmonds is one of the most successful artists of all time. He is a multi-talented musician who writes, sings, produces, plays instruments, and composes. In 1989, he and Antonio "L.A." Reid cofounded LaFace Records, a label within Arista Records. Babyface has worked with many of the biggest names in music today, including Boyz II Men, Toni Braxton, Mariah Carey, Whitney Houston, Madonna, Celine Dion, Aretha Franklin, and Eric Clapton, among many others. He was an executive producer of *My Way*.

## L.A. Reid

L.A. Reid is the man responsible for signing Usher to LaFace. Since that day, the two have formed an inseparable bond. "It's more or less a father-son type thing with me and L.A.," Usher told *Vibe*. "I ain't never really had a father, and L.A. is like a father to me in this industry. I call him Pop." Reid was an executive producer of *My Way*. Like Babyface,

he has a major hand in shaping the careers of all LaFace artists.

## The Notorious B.I.G.

The late artist from Brooklyn is Usher's favorite rapper of all time. With his debut album,

*Ready to Die* (produced by Puff Daddy and released in 1994), The Notorious B.I.G. became one of hip-hop's most popular artists. Unfortunately, his life was cut short when he was shot to death in Los Angeles on March 18, 1997, at the age of 24.

## R. Kelly

Best known for his infectious hit "I Believe I Can Fly," which beat out Usher's "You Make Me Wanna . . ." for a Grammy, Kelly began his recording career in 1992 with R&B group Public Announcement. Since then he has had several hits, including "Sex Me" and "Bump N' Grind." He produced Aaliyah's debut album, *Age Ain't Nothin' but a Number,* in 1994, and has also worked with Michael Jackson—he wrote and coproduced "You Are Not Alone," the second single from Jackson's 1995 *HIStory* album.

## Teddy Pendergrass

After hitting it big in the '70s as the drummer and lead vocalist for Harold Melvin and the Blue Notes, this soul artist went solo in 1976 and had eight hits including "I Don't Love You Anymore," "Close the Door," and "Turn Off the Lights." Tragedy struck when Pendergrass was left partially paralyzed from a car accident. After intense rehabilitation, he returned to music, even making a Top 50 duet with Whitney Houston called "Hold Me" in 1984. He again hit the top of the R&B charts in 1988 with the title track from his *Joy* CD.

# People Are Talking about Usher

**H**ere's what everyone's been saying about this R&B phenom:

"He was good when I first started working with him. But now he's amazing!"

**—Puff Daddy**

"I love your song 'Nice & Slow.' You should do a video for that."

**—Shaquille O'Neal to Usher at the City of Hope National Medical Center fund-raiser in Los Angeles. (Usher had just finished making the video.)**

"The sexiest thing about him is his voice."

**—Supermodel Rebecca Romijn**

"With *My Way,* Usher keeps heading in the right direction."

**—Steve Jones,** *USA Today*

"Dedicated to helping kids in his community, Usher himself is a good role model."

**—Lois Alter Mark,** *Entertainment Weekly*

"'You Make Me Wanna . . .' is the first hit off Usher's upcoming album, and after one look and one listen, Usher will definitely make you wanna do whatever he wants."

*—Fresh!*

"He has a brilliant smile that almost never goes into hiding. He encourages kids to 'put their minds to their dreams.' And he listens to his mother. Is Usher too good to be true? Not by a long shot."
    —**April P. Bernard**, *Teen People*

"The summer heats up with 'You Make Me Wanna . . .' by a not-so-young Usher. . . . The track promises to be a hit among all generations and genders as his loyal young female fan base will eagerly jump aboard."
    —*Billboard*

"Usher continues with the same fiery spirit, endless flow of energy, and that fantastic voice—rhythmic enough to make a deaf woman bob her head. Usher has resurfaced in a major way."
    —*Sister 2 Sister* **magazine**

"Usher comes off like a caring Casanova—one who'll be lying next to you when you wake up in the morning, unless he's downstairs already, *Love Jones* style, scrambling eggs and pouring coffee."
    —**Asondra R. Hunter**, *Vibe*

"Yes, Usher is definitely growing up. He is a young man who is in control of his own destiny and he has surrounded himself with good people to help him along the way. He dreams, then achieves. Like his motto: Strivers achieve what dreamers believe, Usher's dreams will all come true."
    —**Debi Fee**, *Fresh!*

"Next time you're feeling down in the dumps, put that bottle of Tylenol away and try doing things Usher's way."
    —**Elon D. Johnson**, *The Source*

"The singer is quickly emerging as one of the hottest love-men in R&B."
    —*HITS*

"Usher is 'the ultimate entertainer' because of his great voice, fashionable looks, and superstar presence."
    —**Antonio "L.A." Reid**

"For now, Usher is radiating his positive vibe on the Puff Daddy tour, showing the world that there is a lot more to urban music than gangsters and guns."

—*Pollstar*

"There's a lot of competition on the charts, and clearly Usher and his label have come up with what it takes to outdistance it all."

**—*Vibe* editor in chief Danyel Smith**

"Usher more than proved that he is no longer a young boy during his racy set."

**—*Black Beat* magazine on Usher's performance during the Puff Daddy & the Family tour, March 1998**

"He is kind, sincere, and funny."

—*Fresh!*

"Usher's a young buck who's helping to define R&B's new lovey-dovey school."

**—Rick De Yampert, the** *Tennessean*

"He would like the title 'prince of hip-hop swing,' and right now it appears that Usher is on his way."

**—Marc D. Allan, the** *Indianapolis Star*

"You'd have thought *Scream 3* had opened Friday night at Constitution Hall, so loud and frequent was the high-pitched reaction to young R&B heartthrob Usher. Certainly, nineteen-year-old Usher Raymond was doing everything he could to provoke those screams, sometimes through his singing, but just as often through his sensually charged movements. At times, he'd just demand a scream or two from female fans, but mostly Usher worked hard, sang hard, and danced hard to earn them."

**—Richard Harrington, the** *Washington Post*

# Usher on the Web

Usher is all over the Web. Whether you want to see his picture, listen to his music, or hear him being interviewed, it's all just a mouse click away in cyberspace. Here are some of the sites you may want to surf to.

## To Usher, with Love

http://www.idigital.net/pwong/usher.htm

A huge Usher fan from Toronto, Canada, has put together a fun, fact-filled site dedicated to this multitalented star. You'll find up-to-date info, song lyrics, and plenty of photos. You can also sign up to have the site's *Da Usher Connection* newsletter e-mailed to you every week for free. The newsletter includes news, reprints of the latest interviews, a question of the week, and a weekly poll (for example, "Where would you want to go on a date with Usher?") that you can participate in.

## The Unofficial Usher Raymond Home Page

http://www.spods.dcs.kcl.ac.uk/~richii/usher.html

This is a Web site produced in England, so a lot of the info has to do with what Usher has going on in Great Britain. There are lots of photos, a time line (although most of the dates signify something that happened in England), answers to the most frequently asked questions about Usher, and lyrics to many of his songs.

# MTV News Gallery

http://www.mtv.com/news/
gallery/u/usher.html

All of MTV's Web site articles about Usher can be found here. The best is a Q&A between Usher and *MTV News*'s Chris Connelly during Usher's tour with Next and Mary J. Blige. The interview actually took place just ninety minutes before he was going on stage in Universal City, California. Also, there are audio and video clips from the interview.

# Peeps Republic: Usher

http://www.peeps.com/usher/

This hip-hop music site has basic biographical information on Usher. It's a great site to link to other musicians you may be interested in. Also, it provides an easy link to the Web site for *Sister 2 Sister* magazine, an African-American celebrity magazine that has lots of Usher info, too.

# iMusic: Usher

http://imusic.com/showcase/
urban/usher.html

This site has a simple biography and a photo and merchandise for sale. But it provides links to dozens of sites that mention Usher.

# Shiv's Unofficial Usher Homepage

http://www.geocities.com/
Hollywood/Boulevard/7900/

Another fan site with plenty of facts, lyrics, and photos.

# Arista Records: Usher

http://www.aristarec.com/
aristaweb/usher/

This is Usher's record label's official site for him. Again, a simple biography, but excellent audio and video clips. Also, want to know if he's coming to your hometown? Click on "Tour Dates."

# Thirty Must-Know Usher Facts

**1.** He's a Libra--he was born at four A.M. on October 14, 1978, in Dallas, Texas.

**2.** He has a younger brother, James.

**3.** From when he was born until he was twelve, he lived with his mom and brother in Chattanooga, Tennessee. (He has no relationship with his dad.)

**4.** His mom moved the family to Atlanta when he got his recording contract with LaFace Records.

**5.** He loves to shop. On one trip to Atlanta's Lenox Square mall, he bought a pair of Nikes, a jersey, a T-shirt, a baseball cap, and a sweatband for a total of $350--in less than fifteen minutes! And this was after picking up two pairs of sneakers and an Atlanta Braves cap minutes before!

**6.** He has a black Porsche Boxster with a soft peanut-butter color interior. L.A. Reid gave it to him as a gift. Cost? About $50,000.

**7.** He only had three days to prepare his set for the Mary J. Blige tour.

**8.** This star's got a nickname. It's Big Ush.

**9.** His favorite flowers are orchids.

**10.** He's into sports--particularly the Atlanta Hawks.

**11.** If you get to meet him, chances are he'll be wearing his cologne of choice--Amen.

**12.** He has a favorite women's perfume: Spring Fever.

**13.** Usher's got big feet. His shoe size is a 13.

**14.** This future movie star's favorite movie? *The Five Heartbeats,* from 1991.

**15.** When Usher appeared on the Grammys, Calvin Klein insisted he wear his designer threads. There have been reports that Calvin Klein wants Usher to be one of his underwear models.

**16.** Credit his grandmother for getting him to show off his physique. She's the one who told him that he should be flaunting his stuff.

**17.** The only reason "You Make Me Wanna . . ." didn't reach No. 1 was that it came out at the same time as Elton John's "Candle in the Wind" tribute to Princess Diana.

**18.** He has a few different ideal dates. One includes just going to church with a girl, and another is going to a drive-in movie. He'd drop the top of his Porsche so they could watch the movie and the stars.

**19.** He never has to worry about running out of underwear. He owns eighty pairs of Calvins!

**20.** His pet peeve? Usher hates when people grind their teeth.

**21.** You hear Usher's staying at a hotel in your hometown, but when you call they say there's no guest named Usher. Well, try asking for Pepe Le Pu, Ike Turner, or Bill Clinton--he's been known to register at hotels under these aliases.

**22.** He was nominated for a Grammy Award for "You Make Me Wanna . . ." in the category of Best Male R&B Vocal Performance. "It's overwhelming just for my name to be affiliated with the Grammys," he told *Jet*. "I've been working hard toward a goal, and that's to be the ultimate artist. An artist goes for perfection."

**23.** Usher lives for every aspect of music. He's been taking lessons in acoustic guitar and drums.

**24.** Despite Usher's beautifully sculpted body, he's not a complete health freak. He's a sucker for McDonald's and Burger King.

**25.** The craziest thing fans have ever done? Ripped off all Usher's clothes. But Usher sort of started it. "I jumped in the audience, playing. I took off my earrings, my chain, and my watch, and I jumped in the audience and they ripped all my clothes off. . . . I went backstage and put something else on and went back out. I'll never do that again."

**26.** On his next album, he wants to work with R. Kelly and do a duet with Mary J. Blige.

**27.** He feels sexy when he's wearing his white silk robe.

**28.** He loves driving around in his Porsche, but dreams of owning a Bentley one day.

**29.** His favorite clothing lines include Gucci, Polo, Calvin Klein, and Tommy Hilfiger.

**30.** Usher appears in Tommy Hilfiger ads with Kidada Jones, daughter of music icon Quincy Jones.

# Usher has a fan club—of course!

Usher Fan Club
P.O. Box 500338
Atlanta, GA
31150-9998

# How Well Do You Know Usher?

## quiz to find out your Usher IQ.

**1. What is Usher's birthday?**

a. March 11, 1966
b. October 14, 1978
c. January 10, 1970
d. September 30, 1967

**2. What TV show was Usher discovered on?**

a. *Star Search*
b. *Vibe*
c. *Saturday Night Live*
d. *Moesha*

**3. Who did Usher play on *Moesha*?**

a. Q's cousin
b. Moesha's crush, Jeremy, the school football team captain and an aspiring politician
c. Himself, during a concert Moesha went to with Q
d. Moesha's long-lost brother

**4. Which producer loved calling Usher his little brother?**

a. L.A. Reid
b. Babyface
c. Puffy
d. Jermaine Dupri

## 5. After an Usher concert, what are you likely to find on the stage?

a. Usher's shoes, because he says they mark his territory

b. Flowers, because Usher wants the stage to smell nice

c. A picture of Usher as a baby, because he likes to remind his fans where he came from

d. A photo of his mom, to thank her for all her help

## 6. Usher is making his big-screen debut in a film written by the same person who wrote:

a. *Titanic*

b. *Scream*

c. *The Nutty Professor*

d. *Godzilla*

## 7. On what soap opera has Usher appeared?

a. *General Hospital*

b. *Sunset Beach*

c. *The Bold and the Beautiful*

d. *All My Children*

## 8. Which award did Usher win for Best R&B/Soul Single (Male)?

a. A Soul Train Music Award

b. A Grammy

c. An MTV Video Music Award

d. A VH-1 Fashion Award

## 9. What is Usher's favorite song?

a. "Beat It," by Michael Jackson

b. "As We Lay," by Shirley Murdock

c. "I Will Always Love You," by Whitney Houston

d. "My Way," by Frank Sinatra

## 10. Where was Usher born?

a. Atlanta
b. Chattanooga
c. Dallas
d. New York City

## 11. What did LaFace's cofounder Antonio "L.A." Reid give Usher as a gift?

a. A Porsche
b. A beach house
c. A private jet
d. A puppy

## 12. Usher owns at least eighty pairs of what?

a. Air Jordans
b. Calvins
c. Ski pants
d. Sunglasses

## 13. What song did Usher sing when he first performed for LaFace executives?

a. Michael Jackson's "Beat It"
b. Toni Braxton's "Unbreak My Heart"
c. Frank Sinatra's "My Way"
d. Boyz II Men's "End of the Road"

## 14. Who did Usher sing "Slow Jam" with?

a. Brandy
b. Aaliyah
c. Monica
d. Whitney Houston

## 15. What's Usher's nickname?

a. Big Ush
b. Freaky
c. Six-pack Sam
d. Lil' Puffy

Actress Lynn Whitfield and Usher at a benefit concert in New York City.

## 16. What song prevented "You Make Me Wanna . . ." from hitting No. 1 on the pop charts?

a. Puff Daddy's "I'll Be Missing You"
b. R. Kelly's "I Believe I Can Fly"
c. Mase's "What You Want"
d. Elton John's "Candle In the Wind" tribute to Princess Diana

## 17. What was Usher's first television commercial appearance for?

a. Dark & Lovely
b. Michael Jordan's cologne
c. McDonald's
d. Taco Bell

## 18. In what country was the video for "Nice & Slow" shot?

a. England
b. France
c. Spain
d. Italy

## 19. Who encouraged Usher to start taking off his clothes to show off his body?

a. His grandma
b. His backup singers
c. Puffy
d. His brother

## 20. Who did Usher accidentally call "Bill" during the fortieth annual Grammy Awards?

a. Ben Harper
b. Bob Dylan
c. Bobby Brown
d. Busta Rhymes

## 21. What was the name of Usher's only top-ten hit from his first album?

a. "Call Me a Mack"
b. "Nice & Slow"
c. "I'll Be There"
d. "Think of You"

## 22. Who threw a party for Usher during the week of the Grammys in 1998?

a. Mary J. Blige
b. Puffy
c. His mom
d. Mase

## 23. What is Usher's brother's name?

a. James
b. Freddy
c. Josh
d. Will

## 24. Where did Usher take Brandy in Atlanta?

a. An Atlanta Hawks game
b. The Waffle House
c. His mom's house
d. The Coca-Cola bottling plant

## 25. What is Usher's shoe size?

a. 8
b. 9
c. 11
d. 13

# Now add up your score.

| | | | | |
|---|---|---|---|---|
| 1) | a. 1 | b. 4 | c. 3 | d. 2 ❑ |
| 2) | a. 4 | b. 2 | c. 1 | d. 3 ❑ |
| 3) | a. 2 | b. 4 | c. 3 | d. 1 ❑ |
| 4) | a. 2 | b. 1 | c. 4 | d. 3 ❑ |
| 5) | a. 4 | b. 1 | c. 3 | d. 2 ❑ |
| 6) | a. 3 | b. 4 | c. 2 | d. 1 ❑ |
| 7) | a. 2 | b. 1 | c. 4 | d. 3 ❑ |
| 8) | a. 4 | b. 3 | c. 2 | d. 1 ❑ |
| 9) | a. 2 | b. 4 | c. 1 | d. 3 ❑ |
| 10) | a. 2 | b. 3 | c. 4 | d. 1 ❑ |
| 11) | a. 4 | b. 2 | c. 1 | d. 3 ❑ |
| 12) | a. 3 | b. 4 | c. 1 | d. 2 ❑ |
| 13) | a. 2 | b. 1 | c. 3 | d. 4 ❑ |
| 14) | a. 3 | b. 2 | c. 4 | d. 1 ❑ |
| 15) | a. 4 | b. 1 | c. 2 | d. 3 ❑ |
| 16) | a. 3 | b. 2 | c. 1 | d. 4 ❑ |
| 17) | a. 4 | b. 2 | c. 3 | d. 1 ❑ |
| 18) | a. 3 | b. 4 | c. 2 | d. 1 ❑ |
| 19) | a. 4 | b. 2 | c. 3 | d. 1 ❑ |
| 20) | a. 2 | b. 4 | c. 3 | d. 1 ❑ |
| 21) | a. 3 | b. 1 | c. 2 | d. 4 ❑ |
| 22) | a. 2 | b. 4 | c. 3 | d. 1 ❑ |
| 23) | a. 4 | b. 3 | c. 2 | d. 1 ❑ |
| 24) | a. 3 | b. 4 | c. 2 | d. 1 ❑ |
| 25) | a. 1 | b. 2 | c. 3 | d. 4 ❑ |

## TOTAL: ❑

## If you scored:

**25–50 points:** You don't know every single detail about Usher, but that's okay. We know you love his music anyway!

**51–75 points:** You're definitely an Usher fan. You were probably one of the first of your friends to own *My Way*. You won't set your VCR to tape every one of his TV appearances, but you'll drop whatever you're doing if you happen to catch one at the last minute.

**76–100 points:** Congratulations—if there were a Grammy given for Usher's No. 1 Fan, you'd probably have a good shot at taking it home. Maybe you should have written this book.

**Even Salt-N-Pepa can't get enough of Usher, seen here with the group at a benefit concert at New York City's Beacon Theater on December 10, 1997.**

# Discography

## *Usher* (1994)

*Executive Producers:* Sean "Puffy" Combs and Antonio "L.A." Reid

### "I'll Make It Right"

(Darren Benbow, Laquentis Saxon, Kiyamma Griffin, Isaiah Lee, Faith Evans, and Alex Richbourg)
*Producers* . . . Sean "Puffy" Combs and Alex Richbourg

### "Interlude I"

(Faith Evans, Usher, and Carl "Chucky" Thompson)
*Producer* . . . Carl "Chucky" Thompson

### "Can U Get Wit It"

(Devante Swing)
*Producer* . . . Devante Swing

### "Think of You"

(Darnell Jones, Faith Evans, Usher, and Carl "Chucky" Thompson)
*Producers* . . . Sean "Puffy" Combs and Carl "Chucky" Thompson

### "Crazy"

(Brian Alexander Morgan)
*Producers* . . . Brian Alexander Morgan, Sean "Puffy" Combs, and Herb Middleton

### "Slow Love"

(Albert Brown and Isaiah Lee)
*Producers* . . . Al B. Sure!, Kiyamma Griffin, Isaiah Lee, Sean "Puffy" Combs, and Carl "Chucky" Thompson

# Usher appears on these movie sound tracks:
## Poetic Justice, Jason's Lyric, Panther, Kazaam, Soul Food, and Why Do Fools Fall in Love?

**"The Many Ways"**
(Albert Brown and Dave Hall)
*Producers* . . . Dave "Jam" Hall
and Al B. Sure!

**"I'll Show You Love"**
(Mark South, Joe Howell, Faith
Evans, Alex Richbourg, J. Brown,
C. Bobbit, and F. Wesley)
*Producers* . . . Sean "Puffy" Combs
and Alex Richbourg

**"Interlude 2 (Can't Stop)"**
(Faith Evans, Usher, and Carl
"Chucky" Thompson)
*Producers* . . . Sean "Puffy" Combs
and Carl "Chucky" Thompson

**"Love Was Here"**
(Albert Brown and Kiyamma
Griffin)
*Producers* . . . Al B. Sure! and
Kiyamma Griffin

**"Whispers"**
(Devante Swing and Darryl
Pearson)
*Producers* . . . Darryl Pearson and
Devante Swing

**"You Took My Heart"**
(Danielle Jones, Ward Corbett,
Usher, Edward Ferrell, and
Kenneth Torge)
*Producer* . . . Edward "Eddie F"
Ferrell

**"Smile Again"**
*Lyrics by* . . . Dave Hollister, Herb
Middleton, and Faith Evans
*Producers* . . . Sean "Puffy" Combs
and Herb Middleton

**"Final Goodbye"**
(Ward Corbett, Gordon
Chambers, Floyd Norris, and
Dave "Jam" Hall)
*Producer* . . . Dave "Jam" Hall

## My Way (1997)
*Executive Producers:* Antonio
"L.A" Reid, Kenneth "Babyface"
Edmonds, and Jermaine Dupri

**"You Make Me Wanna . . ."**
(Jermaine Dupri, Manuel Seal,
and Usher)
*Producer* . . . Jermaine Dupri

**"Just Like Me"**
(Featuring Lil' Kim)
(Jermaine Dupri, Manuel Seal,
and Lil' Kim)
*Producer* . . . Jermaine Dupri

**"Nice & Slow"**
(Jermaine Dupri, Manuel Seal,
Usher, and Brian Casey)
*Producers* . . . Jermaine Dupri and
Manuel Seal

**"Slow Jam"**
(Featuring Monica)
(Babyface, Belinda Lipscomb, Boaz
Watson, and Sidney Johnson)
*Producer* . . . Babyface

**"My Way"**
(Jermaine Dupri, Manuel Seal,
and Usher)
*Producers* . . . Jermaine Dupri and
Manuel Seal

**"Come Back"**
(Jermaine Dupri, Manuel Seal,
Usher, and Joe Cocker/Chris
Stainton)
*Producers* . . . Jermaine Dupri and
Manuel Seal

**"I Will"**
(T. Riley, C. Hannibal, S. Blair, and
E. Williams)
*Producer* . . . Sprague "Doogie"
Williams

**"Bedtime"**
(Babyface)
*Producer* . . . Babyface

**"One Day You'll Be Mine"**
(Jermaine Dupri, Manuel Seal,
Usher, and the Isley Brothers/C.
Jasper)
*Producers* . . . Jermaine Dupri and
Manuel Seal

**"You Make Me
Wanna . . ."**
(Extended Version)
(Jermaine Dupri,
Manuel Seal, and
Usher)
*Producer* . . .
Jermaine Dupri

# Heaven Sent

## Usher's Career Outlook

If you believe in astrology, you might believe that Usher was born under a lucky star. Noted astrologer Susan Miller believes that's the case with this R&B phenomenon. Here, Miller gives the scoop on Usher's future according to the stars and planets.*

All the stars and planets are in place for Usher to become one of the greatest and most famous entertainers of all time. In order for most performers to leave a mark on the world, they usually have prominent Leos in their chart, and Usher certainly has that. In addition, with Jupiter as the most elevated planet in his chart, Usher will likely have a life full of good fortune, great success, and loads of attention because Jupiter is the planet of luck, growth, achievement, and happiness.

Like many artists, Usher's success is a combination of talent, hard work, and the ability to get along with others. As a typical Libra, he gets along with just about anyone. This trait comes in handy when he's collaborating with lots of different people while working on several projects at one time. With Saturn rising, he's one of the hardest and most responsible workers around. As a Libra, he is quick to give credit to others when credit is due—another reason people like to collaborate with Usher. And since Libras are ruled by Venus, Usher is completely into the arts. He loves things pleasing to the ear and eye. Like his music, Usher wants things smooth and elegant. (Probably no techno stuff will be in Usher's future.)

It should come as no surprise that Usher is in show business. Neptune has a prominent presence in Usher's chart, and

**Usher is a Libra-- he was born October 14, 1978.**

Neptune rules music. Neptune also happens to rule the right side of the brain—the side responsible for all creativity. Usher is very visual, meaning he relates best by seeing ideas and concepts through symbols. That's exactly what much of art and culture does—it gives the world beauty through symbols of powerful acting, dance moves, and musical notes.

With all this love of the arts, it's no wonder Usher has a deep soul and a very strong spiritual side. He's compassionate and would do anything for a friend. He may act macho on the outside (that's because his moon is in Pisces), but he's a softie on the inside.

Although 1997 and 1998 have been great years for Usher, the year 2000—especially July and August—hold even more promise. In fact, Usher isn't even near the peak of his stardom right now. In 2000, he will hit unbelievable milestones.

And with all this fame and fortune, Usher will be able to help out those less fortunate even more than he's already doing now. Since his moon is in Pisces, he has a strong desire to relieve pain and suffering.

## Cosmic Love Connections

What do the stars say about Usher's love life? He gets along well with water signs, like Pisces, Scorpions, Cancers, and

Aquarians because he has five planets in water and he has an earth sign rising (Virgo). Water and earth are always a good mix. This strong buildup of his planets means Usher has a strong emotional side. For example, Usher doesn't like to be persuaded to do things for practical reasons. He doesn't want someone advising him to do something just because it means big bucks. The water signs will agree with Libras like Usher that a person should do something because it means something to him inside— because it strikes an emotional chord.

The kind of woman he goes for is sexy, yet soft. She's poetic and very feminine. In fact, like Usher, she wants to help out the less fortunate. Usher is likely to have a serious relationship with a girl he meets in his neighborhood. He may be introduced to her by a family member or coworker. Since she's likely to be creative and compassionate, she may be a poet, filmmaker, photographer, or even a teacher. And most importantly, she's not about to live her life through Usher. She has amazing self-confidence.

With Usher's moon in the house of committed relationships, he's very devoted to the young women he dates. Yes, he wants to have fun and flirt, but he is also very serious when it comes to relationships. And he expects girlfriends to be committed to him. He definitely doesn't want to hear about dating other guys. But with a strong Scorpio presence, Usher needs some private time all by himself, too.

# Usher's Star Appeal

Although he sometimes likes to be private, Usher is not shy in any way. One look at the stars shows why he loves to show off his body and sing steamy love songs. His Mars, Venus, and Scorpio are conjunct, which means they're all sort of embracing. Mars and Venus are considered the cosmic lovers of the heavens, and they're rarely together in one person's astrological chart. This makes Usher one of the sexiest men around. He's so sexy, he doesn't even have to show off the six-pack. He was born with an aura that drives fans crazy.

So with the stars and planets all in order, expect Usher to be one star who will shine for a long time to come.

*Susan Miller can be reached through her Web site at www.pathfinder.com/twep/astrology/.